# PLANT PETS

## 27 COOL HOUSEPLANTS TO GROW AND LOVE

BY BEATRICE BOGGS ALLEN
*and her mom,*
*Belle Boggs*

Storey Publishing

The mission of Storey Publishing is to serve our customers by
publishing practical information that encourages
personal independence in harmony with the environment.

Edited by Hannah Fries
Art direction by Jessica Armstrong
Book design by Jackie Lay
Text production by Jennifer Jepson Smith

Cover photography by Mars Vilaubi © Storey Publishing,
    except Carey Kirk (authors' photo)
Interior photography by Mars Vilaubi © Storey Publishing
Additional photography by © anjahennern/Shutterstock.com,
    32; Carey Kirk, 36 t.r.; © Dorling Kindersley ltd/Alamy
    Stock Photo, 33 m.; © duncan1890/Getty Images, 12;
    © dvoevnore/Shutterstock.com, 49 t.r.; © Henrik Larsson/
    Shutterstock.com, 33 r.; © K I Photography/Shutterstock
    .com, 54; © Leila Alekto Photo/Shutterstock.com, 53;
    © LorenaEscamilla/Shutterstock.com, 49 b.; © Nancy
    Tripp Photography/Shutterstock.com, 35 r.; © Sofiaworld/
    Shutterstock.com, 41 r.; © Svitlyk/Shutterstock.com, 31
Illustrations by © Aaron Meshon

Storey books may be purchased in bulk for business,
educational, or promotional use. Special editions or book
excerpts can also be created to specification. For details,
please contact your local bookseller or the Hachette Book
Group Special Markets Department at special.markets@
hbgusa.com.

Storey Publishing
210 MASS MoCA Way
North Adams, MA 01247
storey.com

Storey Publishing is an imprint of Workman Publishing,
a division of Hachette Book Group, Inc., 1290 Avenue of
the Americas, New York, NY 10104. The Storey Publishing
name and logo are registered trademarks of Hachette Book
Group, Inc.

Distributed in Europe by Hachette Livre, 58 rue Jean
Bleuzen, 92 178 Vanves Cedex, France
Distributed in the United Kingdom by Hachette Book
Group, UK, Carmelite House, 50 Victoria Embankment,
London EC4Y 0DZ

ISBNs: 978-1-63586-767-1 (paper over board);
978-1-63586-816-6 (ebook)

Printed in China by R. R. Donnelley on paper from
responsible sources

10  9  8  7  6  5  4  3  2  1

RRD-S

Library of Congress Cataloging-in-Publication Data on file

TO MY FRIENDS
AND TEACHERS.
Bea

MINE TOO!
Belle

# CONTENTS

# HELLO FROM BELLE

Bea and I are BIG-TIME ENTHUSIASTS.

We love getting excited about new things. New books, new swimming spots, new mountain-bike trails, new ramen recipes… we're always on the lookout for something to add to our repertoire. Maybe this is why we hardly ever go to pet adoption centers—we'd wind up with a houseful of animals, and for lots of reasons that's just not possible for us.

As Bea's mom, I try to steer her to things we can ENJOY TOGETHER. By the time you read this book, I'm pretty sure Bea will be paddling the small blue kayak I've been saving since before she was born. But sometimes Bea will get into an activity that's far outside my experience or skill set, and I have to watch from the sidelines. I can't stand on my head, horses make me nervous, and I still can't manage a cartwheel. When she fell in love with houseplants, I thought my long history of killing even the hardiest succulents would mean that this would remain her passion, not mine.

But here's the thing about enthusiasm: It's CONTAGIOUS. Watching Bea tend to her little indoor collection, following along as she's found new people to talk to about plants, and helping her research everything from the history of the Hanging Gardens of Babylon to the climate impact of moss has not only been extremely fun, it's also taught me a lot about science, history, and geography.

Taking care of houseplants, or plant pets, as Bea calls them, requires just a little planning and know-how. They're much easier to care for than I expected. (Way easier than a puppy!)

I hope you'll enjoy learning about different kinds of plants, experiments, and crafts from Bea. And then I hope you do what all the plant parents we've met have done for us—SHARE THE LOVE with someone new.

*Belle*

(THE MOM)

# HELLO FROM BEA

Back when I was in kindergarten, at the beginning of the COVID-19 pandemic, my mom brought home some sickly looking plants from her office. They were DROOPY and brown. I hated seeing plants like that, so I rescued them.

I put them on a sunny windowsill in my bedroom. I watered them, I misted them, I checked on them after Zoom school. My mom started bringing home more plants because she noticed that I loved growing them. And so my little garden grew into a MENAGERIE of plants.

In first grade, I adopted *even more plants*, and a wider variety of them. ALOE, I learned, is easy to grow and can be used to treat burns and cuts. A friend who runs a plant nursery gave me a GOLDFISH PLANT whose flowers really look like leaping goldfish. On my birthday, I picked out a MOTH ORCHID with beautiful purple blossoms.

You might think this book is all about houseplants and how to GROW them—and it is—but it's also about finding the plants that *you* love. Plants can clean the air. They make your home pretty, and they're great gifts. You can even sprinkle some of them on pizza or pasta.

I'll teach you how to choose the best plants for your space and your personality, and how to keep your plants happy for a long time. I'll also show you some FUN ACTIVITIES and experiments to do with your plant pets.

I bet you learn so much that you'll be able to teach somebody else about plants!

*Bea*
(THE KID)

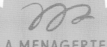

A MENAGERIE (pronounced *muh-NAJ-er-ee*) is a collection of animals, like in a zoo. But the word can also mean an unusual collection of a wide variety of things. That's why I like to say I have a menagerie of plants!

DON'T THEY HAVE PLANT SCIENTISTS AT YOUR SCHOOL?

I WORK IN THE ENGLISH DEPARTMENT, BEA!

THYME

MEET SOME PLANT PETS YOU CAN EAT ON PAGE 42!

SAGE

PARSLEY

MINT

ROSEMARY

SPEARMINT

## PART 1

# GETTING STARTED

So you're thinking of adopting a plant pet! Hurray! There are many reasons to have an indoor garden. Plants add oxygen to the air. They are beautiful and cool. They remind us of nature when we're stuck inside. And it's fun to watch them grow—I get very excited when one of my plants makes a new leaf or a flower.

Plants can also help you make connections with other people. The next time you visit someone who has houseplants, ask them why they have them and where they got them. The answers might surprise you!

# WHERE TO KEEP YOUR PLANT PET

**SO WHERE IN YOUR HOME CAN YOU GROW SOME PLANTS?** Your mom or dad might think the best choice is somewhere close to a sink or the outdoors, or maybe in the living room. But in my experience, the best place for your plant pets to thrive is your bedroom.

Having plants close to where you sleep will remind you to take care of them. I like getting up every morning, walking 3 feet, checking on (and maybe watering) my plants, and then going to eat breakfast and start my day.

Keeping plant pets in your bedroom also helps you appreciate them. You get to move and arrange them how you like, notice new leaves and flowers right away, and enjoy the fresh, clean air they produce.

But if you don't have space or windows in your room, you can try these other places.

- **THE KITCHEN** (great for herbs!)
- **THE LIVING ROOM** (plants make your space look elegant and cool)
- **A PORCH** (when it isn't freezing outside)
- **THE BATHROOM** (Yes, really! Lots of plants like humid spaces.)

GOOD MORNING!

# LET'S DO A LIGHT TEST!

**ALL PLANTS NEED LIGHT,** but they don't all need the same *amount* of light. When you look at plants at a garden center or nursery, you might notice that they are marked with one of the following light ratings.

- Direct light / full sun
- Bright, indirect light
- Medium light
- Low light / shade

Usually this rating will be marked on the small plastic or paper stake that comes with your plant. Keep that stake! It has lots of useful information, including your plant's scientific (Latin) name.

Before you bring home a plant pet, find out what kind of light is in the room where you'll keep your pet so you can make sure it's a good match. Time for a **LIGHT TEST!**

YOU CAN CALL ME TRISH. OR SNAKE PLANT. OR MOTHER-IN-LAW'S TONGUE.

HELLO MY NAME IS DRACAENA TRIFASCIATA

It's best to test the light at the brightest time of day. Place a piece of white paper where you want your plant to go. Then hold your hand over the paper, fingers spread wide.

Look for your hand's shadow. Is it . . .

- Crisp and sharp at the edges? Then you have **DIRECT** light.
- Recognizable as a hand, but kind of fuzzy at the edges? That's bright, **INDIRECT** light.
- A shadow, but you can't count your fingers or see that it's a hand? That's **LOW** light.
- No shadow? You might want to **FIND A DIFFERENT PLACE** for your plant.

## WHO POTTED THE FIRST HOUSEPLANT?

It's hard to say for sure. Scholars believe that BONSAI trees were first potted in China as early as 1000 BCE. And one of the earliest and most famous examples of plants collected for enjoyment and beauty (instead of for food) is the HANGING GARDENS of Babylon, which date back to 600 BCE. According to legend, King Nebuchadnezzar II planted these elaborate potted gardens for his wife, Queen Amytis, who missed the flowers and foliage of her homeland.

# WHAT SUPPLIES DO YOU NEED?

The same way you'd have to get a carrier, leash, and food bowls for a new cat or dog, you'll want to get ready for your plant pet.

What do you need to get started? Not much! All you really *need* is:

- SUNLIGHT
- WATER
- SOIL
- A CONTAINER WITH DRAINAGE

If you want to get fancy, it's nice to have:

- A WATERING CAN with a thin spout (to direct water at the roots)
- A SPRAY BOTTLE or mister to create humidity around your plants (especially good for mosses, orchids, and air plants)
- A SAUCER or a tray to catch any water that drains out of the plant's container
- PERLITE or rice hulls for making your own succulent or cactus soil (you can get them at gardening stores—a bag lasts a long time!)
- FERTILIZER (also lasts a long time, see page 61)

There are lots of ways to cut down on costs. I like to get cute and colorful saucers at the THRIFT STORE, or I scavenge them from my sister's tea sets. (Sorry, Harriet!) You could also get a friend into plant parenting and go halfsies on some of the supplies!

## WHAT DO PLANTS EAT?

Plants get most of what they need from water and sunlight. They take in carbon dioxide from the air, and they get water and nutrients from the air and soil. The CARBON they consume is turned into the energy plants need to grow. Oxygen atoms are released back into the air, making it healthier for us to breathe.

## WHAT'S WITH THOSE ORANGEY-BROWN POTS?

**WHEN YOU GET YOUR PLANT,** it likely will come in a thin plastic container, and you may want to repot it into something sturdier. As the plant grows, sooner or later you will need a new pot to put it in.

The most common kind of pot sold in garden stores is called TERRA-COTTA—it literally means "baked earth," because these pots are made of baked clay. Terra-cotta pots have been used for thousands of years. (The oldest pottery, found in a cave in China, is 20,000 years old.) The pots were initially used for cooking.

At some point, a plant parent must have noticed that terra-cotta pots do a great job of absorbing extra water and letting air and moisture reach the roots of potted plants. That's why you'll see these clay pots everywhere!

# PAINT YOUR TERRA-COTTA POT

Plants add beauty to your bedroom, but what about *their* rooms, otherwise known as their pots? You can decorate plain terra-cotta pots with a few simple supplies and an hour of your time.

## YOU'LL NEED

* Newspaper or cardboard to protect the surface you're working on
* A smock (because acrylic stains!)
* A terra-cotta pot, any size
* Acrylic or craft paint
* Brushes
* Water

1 **COVER** a table or work surface with newspaper or cardboard, and pop on your smock. Set the pot on the paper. **TIP:** It will be easier to paint the pot if you turn it upside down.

2 **PAINT** any design you like, but don't cover the entire surface. Leaving undecorated areas will help the roots and the soil breathe.

3 **FOR A SIMPLE LOOK,** try painting just the rim or making a pattern of dots, stripes, triangles, or other shapes. You could even spatter-paint your pot! (Warning: This is messy.)

4 **LET THE POT DRY.** Then add potting soil and a plant.

# WHERE TO ADOPT

ONE OF THE FIRST PLANT PETS I GOT, after rescuing my mom's half-dead succulents, was easygoing pothos (see page 22). I was tagging along at Get Rooted, the outdoor plant nursery my mom loves, when I saw a little shelf of houseplants. Rudy, one of the garden keepers at Get Rooted, told me that pothos would be easy to take care of. He gave me one of my first plants. I think he could tell I was really interested in taking good care of them.

Houseplant shops are good places to meet plant people and see beautiful plants, but they might be expensive for a kid's budget. Other places to look for plants are hardware stores and grocery stores.

THERE, THERE. GOOD GIRL!

Remember to be respectful and gentle with plants, just like you would with a kitten, a puppy, or an iguana.

MORE TEA, MY DEAR?

To get to know your new plant, I suggest you HOST A TEA PARTY. If you have liquid plant food (see page 61), you can mix it with water and offer a little to your pet. Plain water works, too. Notice how tall your plant is, and how many leaves she has, because guess what? She's gonna grow!

## HOW TO (MAYBE) GET A FREE PLANT

THE SAME WAY YOU MIGHT ADOPT A PET from somebody who has a litter of kittens or puppies, you can also adopt houseplants. The trick is starting conversations with other people, usually grown-ups, which isn't always easy. I was an only child until my sister, Harriet, was born, so I have lots of experience talking to my parents' friends. My best tip is to ASK QUESTIONS. It's more polite to ask other people questions than to just zoom up and start talking about yourself.

Plant people love talking about their plants—and they might just offer you a cutting or two!

Usually, if you start asking questions, plant people will ask you some questions, too. Tell them about your plants, the type of light in your room, and what your GOALS are. You can learn a lot from these conversations! Here are some more examples of what you can ask about, based on your interests.

BEA'S FAVORITE QUESTIONS TO ASK PLANT PEOPLE

1. What is your favorite plant? Why?
2. How did you get into plants?
3. Have you ever killed a plant? Have you ever saved one?

\* DO YOU LIKE FAST-GROWING PLANTS? *Ask which plants grow fastest and how to encourage growth.*

\* ARE YOU DRAWN TO COLOR OR FLOWERS? *Ask if they have any easy-growing, flowering plants. Hint: Ask about begonias!*

\* ARE YOU HOPING TO SHARE YOUR PLANTS WITH FRIENDS? *Ask which plants are easiest to propagate, or raise babies from.*

# PET-SAFE PLANT PETS

**DO YOU ALREADY HAVE AN ANIMAL PET** (like a cat or dog)? Then you need to be careful to select pet-safe plant pets. (Try saying that three times fast!)

We have two indoor-outdoor cats, Julius and Coco, and I would never want to hurt them! I asked their vet, Dr. Cindi Baucom, if there are any plants I need to AVOID.

For cats, Dr. Cindi says that the most toxic plants are LILIES—particularly Easter lilies, tiger lilies, Japanese show lilies, Stargazer lilies, rubrum lilies, and daylilies.

Cats can get kidney failure by eating any part of the plant, or even by drinking lily pollen from a saucer's water. "I would absolutely avoid any type of lily plant if you have cats in the household," she advises.

For dogs, the most toxic plants are SAGO PALMS, Dr. Cindi told us. "This includes cycads, Japanese cycads, coontie palms, and cardboard palms. All parts of the plants are toxic, but especially the seeds." These plants can cause liver failure in dogs.

Other plants, like POINSETTIAS, PHILODENDRON, and POTHOS, can irritate both cats and dogs. These plants won't send your pet to the hospital, but it makes sense to keep them out of reach.

# WHERE A LOVE OF PLANTS CAN TAKE YOU

FOR SOME PEOPLE, CARING FOR PLANT PETS ISN'T JUST A HOBBY—IT'S THEIR JOB! Read about farmer Patricia Parker on page 44, orchid grower Jeff Baldwin on page 55, and horticulture student Andrew Pfeifer on page 66. You can even become a doctor of plants, like our friend Anju Manandhar!

## LIFE OF A PLANT SCIENTIST

Dr. Anju Manandhar spends her days in greenhouses, surrounded by plants. How did she get to this DREAM LIFE? She says that one day she was walking by the agronomy building at North Carolina State University and decided to go inside. She'd always been interested in plants and wanted to help people around the world grow food. She especially wanted to help people in Nepal, the country where she was born. Anju got a job working in the agronomy lab, and the rest is history!

Now Anju has a doctorate in plant physiology and studies how ferns and mosses take in water through their stomata (tiny holes in their leaves). Learning how plants get the right amounts of water and carbon can help farmers ADAPT to changing environments.

## CLASSIFY YOUR PLANTS

MOST COMMON HOUSEPLANTS ARE FLOWERING PLANTS, OR ANGIOSPERMS. These can be divided into two main groups—monocots and dicots. Monocots have one leaf inside their seed, and dicots have two. Monocots have many thready roots and are fast growing. Dicots have a taproot, which is a single thick root that grows deep in the soil.

MONOCOT          DICOT

"WHAT ABOUT FERNS?" you might ask. Have you ever seen a flower on a fern? Nope! That means that these plants aren't angiosperms. They reproduce with spores, like mushrooms.

TURN A MOSS
TERRARIUM INTO
A TINY MAGICAL
WORLD
(PAGE 50)!

## PART 2

# COOL PLANT PETS!

I have 38 pets in my bedroom—that number of cats or dogs or birds or hamsters would never fit, but plants are much easier to take care of, so my mom says the more the merrier. Which is good news since I'm always getting new ones. I have a hanging fern and a crocodile fern, two pothos, three orchids, a bunch of succulents, two begonias, two air plants, and more! Read on to learn about some of my favorites.

# POTHOS
## PLANT PETS BY THE FOOT

**HOW ABOUT A PLANT THAT CAN GROW MORE THAN A FOOT A MONTH WHILE YOU BASICALLY IGNORE IT?** Just kidding! We know you want to take great care of your new pets, but if you're just getting started or you have a busy schedule, pothos might be the pet for you.

This plant pet is great for beginners because even under not-perfect conditions (like low light or slightly chilly temperatures), it won't die. It'll just grow more slowly. But keep this plant happy, and you'll have lots of new, pretty greenery to enjoy.

Pothos, named after a Greek god of desire, has heart-shaped leaves that can seem to reach for you.

In the right conditions, the long stems can grow 18 inches a month, twisting around your bedroom.

This is a leaf node. Pothos can grow new roots from these nodes!

## ABOUT THIS PET

**CHALLENGE LEVEL:** 🌿 🌿 🌿 🌿 🌿

😊 **LIKES:** Bright, indirect light; warm temperatures

☹ **DISLIKES:** Direct sun, cold temperatures

**ALSO KNOWN AS:** Devil's ivy, money plant

**NATIVE TO:** Southeast Asia

**BEST FOR:** Newbies, interior decorators

## SHARE THE LOVE

It's easy to grow a new pothos from a **CUTTING** taken from a healthy plant, and the resulting baby plant makes a great gift for a friend.

Snip off a healthy vine about a quarter inch before a leaf node. The **LEAF NODE** is a small bump in the branch or vine, where roots will grow from the new plant. Fill a small glass jar or plastic bottle with water, plop the clipping inside, and set it on a windowsill with bright, indirect light. Change the water every week, and watch as roots grow! Once you see some thready roots, you can plant your new pet into a pot with potting soil.

**TIP:** The best kind of water to use for propagating plants is what they'd get in nature— rainwater! Simply set a large jar or watering can outside when you know it might rain. (If you have a rain barrel, even better!)

# HOW TO TRAIN YOUR POTHOS

Like a good pet, pothos can be trained. Try coaxing your viny pet into climbing a bookcase or winding around a window frame.

### YOU'LL NEED

* A mature pothos plant
* Scissors
* String
* Supports to tie the pothos to, like adhesive hooks, a bed frame, or (my personal choice) pushpins

1  Find a long pothos vine and carefully EXTEND it without breaking it or lifting its roots from the soil.

2  PRUNE away any side branches if necessary, and use string to tie the main vine gently to your support.

3  As the plant grows, TIE the extra lengths to the next location where you want the plant to climb.

4  Keep the pothos FED, adding water mixed with fertilizer once a month or so during the spring and summer. (Read about the Persephone period on page 46.)

Try these other fast-growing, easygoing pets.

## NEON POTHOS

*Neon* is the word—this pothos is bright green and easy to care for.

## PHILODENDRON

So pretty! Choose between vining and upright varieties.

## SPIDER PLANT

Perfect for a humid bathroom with plenty of light. Trim its hanging babies and plant their roots in the soil to grow more!

## PRAYER PLANT

This pet will close its leaves at night like praying hands.

# MOTHER OF THOUSANDS

## SO. MANY. PLANT. BABIES.

Plantlets, a.k.a. plant babies!

**IF YOU WANT A THOUSAND**—or at least a few dozen—new plant pets, then mother of thousands is the perfect pet for you.

I got my first mother of thousands plant at the farmers' market, but soon I had many more—so many that I had to scramble to find new homes for them. That's just about the only thing that makes this cool, productive succulent a challenge—keeping up with those BABIES!

Plantlets fall to the soil and grow more plant pets!

## PLANTLETS GALORE

Mother of thousands grows amazingly fast and performs a cool MAGIC TRICK, growing tiny versions of herself on her leaves. When they grow too big or get bumped, they fall into the soil, take root, and grow. In fact, they grow their threadlike roots even while they're attached to their mom. We call these babies PLANTLETS.

When they're about an inch tall, I pluck them from the mother's soil and put them into new pots with good drainage. When they reach 3 or 4 inches tall, they start growing babies of their own.

These wide, thick leaves store lots of water. Mother of thousands doesn't need to be watered often, so be sure to wait until the soil dries out.

## ABOUT THIS PET

CHALLENGE LEVEL:

😊 LIKES: Filtered to bright, indirect light; good drainage (use cactus or succulent soil)

☹️ DISLIKES: Too much water, too much direct sun (which can burn her leaves)

ALSO KNOWN AS: Devil's backbone, Mexican hat plant, alligator plant

NATIVE TO: Madagascar

BEST FOR: Gift givers, aspiring propagators

# PLANT-PET PARTY FAVORS!

Plantlets make a unique, eco-friendly party favor, and mother of thousands is one of the easiest plants to share. I did this at my eighth birthday party, and my friends loved it! (See page 15 for how to paint a terra-cotta pot—another great party activity.)

## YOU'LL NEED

* Succulent potting mix (see page 60 for how to make your own)
* Small containers or peat pots
* A healthy mother of thousands plant with plantlets
* Tweezers (optional)
* Water
* A mister (optional)
* Friends!

1 GATHER your supplies and friends (working outdoors is best). Tell them about the amazing mother of thousands plant, including how she came from Madagascar and will make So! Many! Babies!

2 Have each friend SCOOP some cactus potting mix into a container.

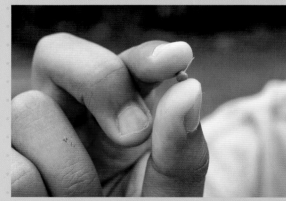

3 Show your friends how to PLUCK a plantlet carefully from the mom's leaves, bringing the threadlike roots along. You might want to use tweezers for this task.

4 NESTLE the plantlet on top of the soil, and water carefully to moisten the soil. If you have a mister, you can use that, too. Tell your friends to put their new plants in a sunny window and prepare to be amazed.

## A MOTHER ON THE MOVE

Mother of thousands is native to MADAGASCAR, home of lemurs and many other unique creatures and plants, but humans have taken this succulent all over the world. She grows so well that if you live where outdoor temperatures never fall below freezing, you should probably keep her indoors so that she doesn't crowd out native plants.

## IF YOU LIKE MOTHER OF THOUSANDS . . .

Here are other succulents that are easy to propagate.

### STRING OF PEARLS

Snip a strand below a leaf node and strip a few pearls from the cut end. Make a small hole and plant the stem.

### JADE

You can grow a new jade plant from a single leaf. Simply lay the leaf on top of the potting mix and water occasionally until the leaf sprouts little roots!

### TEDDY BEAR SUCCULENT

Cut a stem from this plant and let it sit a few days. Then simply plant it!

### ALOE VERA

See page 38 for more about this healing plant and how to propagate it.

# VENUS FLYTRAP

## THIS PLANT EATS WHAT??

**VENUS FLYTRAPS ARE CARNIVOROUS PLANTS!** That means they get some of their nutrition from insects, which they trap by snapping their leaves shut around unlucky flies, ants, spiders, and mosquitoes.

I named my flytraps Trappy and Trappy 2.0. These plants can be a little DRAMATIC. During their growing season (spring and summer), Venus flytraps love sun and hate cold weather—even air-conditioning bothers them! So during summer, I take Trappy outside where she can get lots of humid, warm air—and also catch some BUGS!

Don't touch your flytrap's trigger hairs. That could cause her to waste precious energy.

If leaves blacken and die (which is normal during dormancy), pinch them off. New ones should grow back during the growing season.

Set your flytrap's pot in a tray or dish that can hold water. Keep the tray filled about ½ inch deep with rainwater or distilled water.

Believe it or not, the fly-chomping Venus flytrap was named after the Roman goddess of love because of the plant's beautiful white flowers, which bloom in spring.

## ABOUT THIS PET

**CHALLENGE LEVEL:** 🍃🍃🍃🍃🍃

😊 **LIKES:** Full sun, warm temperatures, eating bugs

☹️ **DISLIKES:** Cold!

**NATIVE TO:** Eastern North and South Carolina (not too far from where I live!)

**BEST FOR:** Adventurous plant parents

## HOW TRAPPY CATCHES DINNER

If your Venus flytrap sits in a dish of water, the water can help trap a bug by acting as a MOAT. Just set a live ant on the soil. The ant won't be able to climb over the water and eventually it'll trigger the flytrap's jaws. CHOMP! Here's how Trappy gets her meal.

**1** She releases a fruity scent from her hinged leaves, attracting nearby insects.

**2** An insect lands on her leaf, ruffling Trappy's highly sensitive CILIA (trigger hairs).

**3** When the hairs are triggered, SNAP! She closes the leaf over the insect.

**4** Her strong cilia hold the insect in place. Over the next 5 to 12 days, she releases digestive juices that consume the bug.

**5** Once she's taken in all the nutrition she can get, the leaf opens again, ready for more PREY.

# BE A WILD PLANT ADVOCATE

Did you know that many beloved plants, including the Venus flytrap, are vulnerable or ENDANGERED in the wild? The biggest threat to the Venus flytrap is habitat loss, caused by development, deforestation, and climate change. Find out more about how you can help protect the flytrap's habitat by connecting with the North Carolina Coastal Land Trust. They host an annual FLYTRAP FROLIC, with tours of a flytrap garden plus educational activities.

You can also send your congressperson an email or letter. Tell your representative why you think it's important to protect the native habitats of wild plants in your state. To learn more about NATIVE PLANTS where you live, look up your state's native plant society, ask your librarian to help you find a book on the subject, or visit the Center for Plant Conservation's endangered plant finder at saveplants.org.

## BIG APPETITE

There are more than 600 different kinds of MEAT-EATING plants in the world. The largest one is called the giant montane pitcher plant. Its pitcher trap can hold almost a gallon of liquid, which it uses to digest small animals, including MAMMALS (!) that fall in.

HEY LITTLE MOUSY, NEED A BATH?

## IF YOU LIKE VENUS FLYTRAP . . .

Try these other carnivorous plants.

### PITCHER PLANT

Makes a good hanging plant! Dislikes the cold but loves damp soil.

### COBRA LILY

These plants like lots of moisture and do well in sunny bathrooms.

### SUNDEW

Keep your sundew in a sunny window in your kitchen. It will eat gnats!

# AIR PLANT

## NO SOIL? NO PROBLEM!

TILLANDSIA CAPUT-MEDUSAE

THIS IS ONE OF THE CUTEST PLANT PETS. My favorite air plant is called *Tillandsia ionantha*. With its spiky leaves, it looks like a deep-sea creature. Air plants don't even need dirt to grow because they get all their nutrients from the air! In the wild, they normally grow on trees. Like pothos and mother of thousands, air plants are easy-to-care-for, chill plant pets.

But unless you live in the tropics, where the climate is HUMID all the time, you'll need to do *some* work to make your air plant happy. Air plants need frequent spritzing and love. Luckily, it's not hard to love them—just look at those little guys!

Mist around your air plant two or three times a week, especially in winter when the air may be cool and dry.

Watch out for mushy roots! If roots get soft, let them dry out and mist or dunk your plant less often.

TILLANDSIA IONANTHA

Once a week, dunk your plant in room-temperature water, preferably rainwater. (Chlorinated water can harm the plant.)

**CHALLENGE LEVEL:**

😊 **LIKES:** Bright or filtered indirect light, good airflow, humidity and weekly baths

☹ **DISLIKES:** Being cooped up or enclosed in glass jars, cold or dry air

**NATIVE TO:** Tropical Central America and Mexico

**BEST FOR:** Neat freaks

**ALSO KNOWN AS:** Sky plant, air fern

## WHAT'S AN EPIPHYTE?

Air plants are closely related to orchids. Air plants and many orchids are EPIPHYTES! An epiphyte is a plant that attaches to another plant (like a tree) for support, taking all its nutrients from the air and rainwater. Unlike parasites, epiphytes don't hurt their host.

If you've ever been in a tropical or subtropical place and looked closely at the trees, you've probably seen epiphytes. Beautiful, spooky SPANISH MOSS is neither Spanish nor a moss, but it is a type of epiphyte!

# CREATIVE CONTAINERS

Because air plants don't need soil, you can get creative with their containers. Try wiring an air plant to a piece of driftwood or a thick piece of tree bark, where she'll eventually take root. Or look for cute TEACUPS or other vessels to hold her.

Be creative! I found a tiny ceramic globe for Misty at a thrift store for 50 cents! She sits in the top, her leaves curling around the edges like a giant squid!

Bzzzz

I made my mom a clay pinch-pot vase in the shape of our cat Julius's head. She thought it would make a funny container for an air plant—and she was right! The air plant looks just like wild green hair.

## ONE CHANCE TO BLOOM

Many air plants come in beautiful colors, and if you take *very* good care of your air plant, you will eventually see something special: It will BLOOM. This happens only once in the plant's lifetime and will result in something even more special: PUPS. Yes, air plant babies are called pups, and they can be separated from the mother plant once they are one-third her size (or leave them attached to mama to form a clump).

My air plant, Misty, hasn't bloomed yet, but when she does, I will be careful not to submerge her flower in water so it doesn't rot.

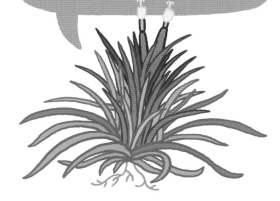

I DON'T NEED MUCH, DAHLING... JUST A SPRITZ NOW AND THEN, A WEEKLY RAINWATER BATH, SOME NICE WARM AIR...

## IF YOU LIKE *TILLANDSIA IONANTHA* . . .

Try these other species of air plants.

### TILLANDSIA TECTORUM

Can you guess why this is also called a snowball air plant?

### TILLANDSIA XEROGRAPHICA

This one is sometimes called the King of Air Plants because it gets much bigger than most.

### TILLANDSIA CAPUT-MEDUSAE

I've never seen one of these in person, but I'd love to have a plant named after the Greek monster Medusa!

# ALOE VERA

## A MEDICINE CABINET ON YOUR WINDOWSILL

There are more than 500 species of aloe plants. Wild aloe vera can live for 100 years or longer!

**HAVE YOU EVER WANTED TO HEAL PEOPLE WITH THE SNAP OF A LEAF?** With aloe vera, a kind of flowering succulent, you can do just that!

I don't recommend eating aloe vera, but it's great to have on hand as a TOPICAL treatment (that means something you put right on your skin) for burns, cuts, and sunburns. My mom sometimes burns herself cooking, and my aloe vera plant has come to the rescue many times.

These thick leaves store a lot of water. Aloe needs watering only once every two or three weeks.

## ABOUT THIS PET

**CHALLENGE LEVEL:** 🍃🍃🍃🍃🍃

🙂 **LIKES:** Bright or filtered sun to full sun

😦 **DISLIKES:** Being outside in the cold, sitting in water

**NATIVE TO:** Africa and the Arabian Peninsula

**BEST FOR:** Aspiring doctors and nurses (or slime enthusiasts), forgetful types

Big fat leaves can grow heavy and lopsided. To help your plant grow in a balanced way, put it in a sunny spot and rotate it every few days so that all the leaves get plenty of sun.

# PROPAGATING ALOE VERA

Like air plants (see page 34), aloe vera produces little PUPS—just way more often! An aloe pup looks like a small version of its mom, growing close to the main plant.

To propagate your aloe (and maybe share with a friend), just reach into the soil and gently pull out the pup, leaving as much stem and root intact as you can.

Pack some succulent or CACTUS SOIL (see page 60) into a terra-cotta pot, use your finger to make a hole in the soil deep enough for the roots, and insert the pup, letting the leaves poke up.

TIP: If your aloe pup wants to fall over, prop it up with a layer of small rocks on top of the soil.

1

2

3

## GREEN IDEA

# MAKE YOUR OWN ALOE VERA GEL

You know that bright green sunburn gel sold at the supermarket every summer? You can make your own if you have an aloe plant or two. It won't be bright green, but it'll work just as well.

**YOU'LL NEED**

* A thick aloe vera leaf
* A paring knife
* A clean cutting board
* A regular spoon
* A small glass jar with a lid

1 Choose a thick, healthy leaf and SNAP it off with your fingers.

2 Using the knife and cutting board, CUT off the bottom and top tip of the leaf. Then TRIM away the spiky sides. You should see a thick, juicy layer of clear gel in the middle—kind of like a slime sandwich!

3 Next, SLICE off one side of the outer skin (you can compost the skin).

4 Using the spoon, SCRAPE the gel onto the cutting board, then scoop it into the jar and attach the lid. STORE the gel in the fridge and use it for burns, small cuts, and sunburn.

## ANCIENT BEAUTY

Aloe vera has been used as a medicine and beauty product for thousands of years. It was traded on the SILK ROAD, where it was valued as a treatment for wounds, burns, and fevers. According to legend, CLEOPATRA used aloe vera as part of her beauty routine. It keeps skin soft and smooth and helps prevent scars.

## IF YOU LIKE HEALING WITH PLANTS . . .

You might like growing these other medicinal herbs, which can be steeped in hot water to make tea.

### PEPPERMINT

To help digestion or soothe a stomachache, you can make tea or just pop a leaf in your mouth and chew on it after a meal.

### LEMON BALM

Crush a few leaves and smell them when you're feeling anxious or upset—the aroma can help calm you down.

### CHAMOMILE

The flowers are famous for making a calming bedtime tea. Hey, it worked for Peter Rabbit!

# THE INDOOR HERB GARDEN

## EAT YOUR PETS

**DO YOU LOVE TO COOK?** Then you probably know that herbs are great for adding extra FLAVOR to dishes like pizza, pasta, and ramen (my favorite). It might seem weird to get plant pets just to eat them, but don't worry—with the right care, these pets keep growing!

Small potted herb plants are easy to come by at grocery stores and garden centers, and you can keep them indoors or out, if the weather is warm. They may get crowded in their plastic pots. Divide and replant them to give their roots room to spread out.

Start with one or two herbs and add more to your indoor garden once you've got the hang of it. Some EASY and TASTY herbs to start with are mint, sweet basil, parsley, chives, and thyme.

**BASIL**
Pinch off new growth (sprinkle it on pizza!) and snap off any flowers. Once it flowers, it will stop growing.

**ROSEMARY**
Use cactus potting mix and make sure the soil dries out before watering it again.

**THYME**
Try different varieties! Lemon thyme smells amazing.

**CHALLENGE LEVEL:** Depends on the herb! Basil needs a lot of sun, so we give it a 4. Mint is famous for growing just about anywhere, so it gets a super-easy 1.5.

**LIKES:** Indirect to direct light, good soil drainage

**DISLIKES:** North-facing windows, soggy soil, cold weather

**NATIVE TO:** Many popular cooking herbs are native to Asia and the Mediterranean

**BEST FOR:** Chefs, foodies

## SEARCHING FOR SUN

Give your herbs the **SUNNIEST** spot you can! My house is pretty shady, so during summer months, I plant my herbs in a small wagon that I can move from sunny patch to sunny patch.

**PARSLEY**
Choose between flat-leaf or curly! This easy herb needs a nice deep container for its long root.

# MAKE HERB SALT!

Most of the vegetables and herbs my family uses come from In Good Heart Farm, a nearby farm run by Ben Shields and Patricia Parker and their two kids. We are so grateful to them for growing our food!

Sometimes Patricia makes a delicious herb salt we like to sprinkle on POPCORN and PIZZA, so we asked her for a recipe. She recommends the combinations below, but you can also experiment with what you have, asking your parents for some of the dried herbs in your pantry. Remember that you can always add MORE of an ingredient, but you can't take it away once it's added.

* ITALIAN: Rosemary, sage, and thyme
* RANCH: Dill, parsley, and onion powder
* CHIMICHURRI: Parsley, garlic powder, red pepper flakes, and a few gratings of lemon zest

## YOU'LL NEED

* 2 large bunches of fresh herbs of your choice (each bunch should be about the same size as a bunch of parsley you would get at the store)
* ½ cup Maldon finishing salt or coarse sea salt
* Onion powder, garlic powder, or red pepper flakes (optional)
* A food processor or blender
* A glass jar or small metal containers

Tie a pretty RIBBON around your jar and give it as a gift to the chefs in your life!

1 The first step is to **DRY** your herbs. You can do this one of two ways. Tie the stems together with twine, and **HANG** the bunches in a corner of the kitchen. Or **LAYER** the stems between paper towels, then leave them at room temperature. Either way, most herbs will take 5 to 10 days to dry until crumbly.

2 **BLEND** the salt, ½ cup of the dry herbs, and any other ingredients you choose in the food processor or blender.

3 **POUR** the mixture into the jar for gifting. Let the flavors meld for a few hours, or even a few days, before using. You don't have to remove the stems unless you want to.

# AVOID THE PERSEPHONE PERIOD

In Greek mythology, Persephone was the daughter of Demeter, the goddess of the HARVEST. She was kidnapped by Hades, the god of the underworld. Because he tricked her into eating some pomegranate, the fruit of the underworld, Persephone had to stay with him for part of the year. This is winter, when Demeter does not let crops grow because she misses Persephone.

Farmers and gardeners know the time of year when the sun shines for fewer than 10 hours a day as the "Persephone period." Most crops won't actively grow during this time. The same is true for houseplants—especially herbs! So don't try to start them from seeds or seedlings during this period. They also need less water and no fertilizer. It's their time of dormancy and REST.

Here is the Persephone period for a few US cities, but you can look up your own online.

* Boston, MA      November 8–February 1
* Washington, DC      November 17–January 23
* Pittsboro, NC      November 30–January 13
* Atlanta, GA      December 6–January 4

## WHAT MAKES A PLANT AN HERB?

BOTANISTS (scientists who study plants) define herbs as seed-bearing plants that don't have a woody stem and that die to the ground in winter. But you can also think of herbs as leafy plants that have a USEFUL PURPOSE.

Herbs have been used by people around the world for thousands of years. Ancient Egyptians studied and used herbs in MEDICINE and religious ceremonies way back in 3500 BCE! Traditional Chinese medicine, which has been practiced for at least 2,300 years, prescribes herbs to BALANCE the body's energies and heal different sicknesses. Herbs and herb seeds have even been depicted in ancient cave paintings.

THIS PLACE COULD REALLY USE SOME AIR FRESHENER...

## STOP THE STINK!

If you lived in sixteenth- or seventeenth-century England, you could have worked as a ROYAL HERB STREWER! Kings and queens hired these people to scatter herbs and flowers in their apartments to cover up stinky smells coming from city streets.

## IF YOU LIKE EXPERIMENTING WITH HERBS . . .

Here are some other herbs to smell, taste, and enjoy.

### CATNIP

Grows best in direct light, with well-drained soil—and is sure to make your cat happy (if you have one).

### LAVENDER

Needs six hours of direct sun or a grow light. Best as a plant that lives outdoors in summer and indoors in winter.

### SAGE

Another tasty aromatic herb that likes plenty of sun. Like lavender, it can live outdoors in summer and indoors in winter. Add it to your Thanksgiving stuffing!

# MOSS

## YOUR SOFTEST, FUZZIEST PLANT PET

**Mist your moss often to keep it moist!**

**WHAT'S SPECIAL ABOUT MOSSES?** Just about everything! Don't overlook this OG (original ground) plant. The next time you're taking a walk outside, look for moss. You might find it on trees, rocks, even the sides of brick buildings or in the cracks of sidewalks. My sister, Harriet, and I love to pet mosses on our walks.

Did you know that you can tame moss and keep it indoors with your other plant pets? We realized this when we found some old glass bottles filled with moss in the woods—accidental TERRARIUMS! Some people like to add moss to orchid and bonsai pots, too.

**Keep your moss garden somewhere you'll remember to check on it.**

## ABOUT THIS PET

**CHALLENGE LEVEL:**

🙂 **LIKES:** Moisture, rocks, tree bark

☹️ **DISLIKES:** Direct sunlight, dry conditions

**NATIVE TO:** The whole planet! Mosses grow just about anywhere, even in hot desert landscapes and freezing Antarctica.

**BEST FOR:** Artists, playful types, budding landscape architects

If you live in a very dry place, add a lid or plastic wrap to keep moisture inside (but make sure air can get in).

## COOL FACTS ABOUT MOSS

Moss is amazing! Here are a few things that make this plant pet unique.

* Mosses were the very **FIRST** plants on Earth! Today there are more than 12,000 different kinds of moss.

* Many moss leaves are just one **CELL** thick. Use a magnifying glass to get a close-up look at your moss.

* Because moss isn't a **VASCULAR** plant (meaning it doesn't have veins that carry water), it can't grow tall. It gets its nutrients from sunlight, dew, air, and rain.

* Mosses remove and store more carbon from the atmosphere than all the trees in the world. Some cities are planting **VERTICAL** moss gardens as a way of cleaning the air.

* In Japan, moss is used to make beautiful hanging planters called **KOKEDAMA**. The art of kokedama is centuries old. *Koke* means "moss," and *dama* means "ball."

# MAKE A TERRARIUM

DON'T STOMP ON YOUR **ELDERS!**

A moss terrarium is a fun way to create a tiny world in a jar. A canning jar makes a nice home for your mossy pet. We've also had good luck using glass vases from the thrift store.

## YOU'LL NEED

- ✴ Moss (collect a few different varieties)
- ✴ A handful of small rocks or pebbles
- ✴ A widemouthed glass jar or a repurposed glass vase
- ✴ Potting soil or a little soil from where you found your moss
- ✴ A spray bottle
- ✴ Decorative accessories (optional)

**1** **COLLECT** your moss and rocks. Harriet and I used rocks from our yard and moss we found near a stream. We only took a little moss because it's part of the ecosystem, and we don't want to mess that up!

**2** **COVER** the bottom of the terrarium jar with a layer of rocks. **SPRINKLE** a little soil on top.

**3** **PLACE** the moss, and any sticks or soil the moss clings to, on top of the soil.

**4** **SPRAY** with water until the moss glistens with droplets, like it would after a rain.

Ferns and mosses are older than dinosaurs. They grew before any flower ever bloomed on Earth, and their ancient fossils got compressed underground into coal and oil.

5 **ACCESSORIZE!** You can add other plants, sticks, or pretty rocks. I made a tiny snail out of clay and added it. Harriet put a small plastic guinea pig and some fairies in her garden. Or enjoy your moss as is.

6 Set your terrarium in a spot that receives at least 6 hours of bright, **INDIRECT SUNLIGHT** a day. Keep the spray bottle nearby so you'll remember to mist.

# IF YOU LIKE MAKING TERRARIUMS . . .

Here are some other plants that like damp environments.

## TINY FERNS

Look around for little ferns near the place where you collect your moss. Or find small varieties at plant stores, such as the lemon button fern or fluffy ruffles fern.

## CARNIVOROUS PLANTS

Venus flytraps or sundew will do well in a terrarium. Leave the lid open regularly to make sure insects can get in.

# MOTH ORCHID

## YOUR SHOWIEST PET

ON MY EIGHTH BIRTHDAY, MY MOM TOOK ME ON A SECRET ERRAND —she wouldn't tell me where we were going, and I wondered: *Was it a toy store? An indoor swimming pool?* We soon pulled up to an ordinary-looking house and parked near some greenhouses. "Surprise!" my mom said. "We're at the ORCHID GALLERY."

This place was way more magical than a toy store. Two connected greenhouses held more than 4,000 plants, some of them colorful with flowers, others green and lush.

The orchid I'd recommend for BEGINNERS is one I picked out that day: the moth orchid. It's the most common orchid sold in stores. Don't be nervous about raising an orchid! Just find the right throne for your princess and keep her watered.

The moth orchid's scientific name, *Phalaenopsis*, means "mothlike" because her flowers look like moths. They last for up to three months!

Node, where new growth can occur

Roots

Planting medium

When my orchids finish blooming, I cut the stem close to the base. This helps the plants conserve energy so they can bloom again.

Aerial roots absorb water from the air through a spongelike covering called the velamen. (Never cut these wandering roots because they help your orchid get nutrients.)

CHALLENGE LEVEL:

 **LIKES:** Bright, indirect light; humid air; regular pruning; special planting medium

**DISLIKES:** Too much water, cold air

**NATIVE TO:** Every continent except Antarctica!

**BEST FOR:** Flower lovers, patient types, experienced plant parents

## WHAT'S WITH THE SPECIAL PLANTING MEDIUM?

Orchids don't sit inside a regular terra-cotta pot filled with regular potting soil, like your other plant pets. An orchid's throne is a clear plastic pot filled with a **PLANTING MEDIUM** suited to your type of orchid. A moth orchid's planting medium would be a mix of bark, perlite, peat, and sphagnum moss. This special way of being planted mimics, or copies, how an orchid grows in nature.

In the wild, most orchids grow on trees because they are epiphytes (see page 35). They often hang upside down because their flowers are so heavy. They gather nutrients and moisture from the tropical air.

Imagine watering orchids as if you're a rainstorm—they need an occasional good **SOAKING,** and then time for their roots to dry out.

# KEEP YOUR PRINCESS HAPPY!

Let me pass along a few tips about these regal companions (my orchids don't like to be called pets) . . .

- CHOOSE A PLANT WITH LOTS OF BUDS. Choose orchids with only a few or no blooms, just buds. That way you can enjoy your blooms for longer, and you get to watch them open.

- GIVE IT GOOD LIGHT. Your orchid will do best in a spot where she has some good light but isn't in direct sunlight. Good orchid light means that you can make a shadow (fuzzy or crisp) for at least four hours a day. Don't put an orchid near an air vent.

- WATER WHEN LIGHT. A good way to tell whether your orchid needs to be watered is by testing the weight. If the plant feels light, then it probably needs water. If it feels heavy, it should be good a while longer. You also might want to think about watering if the top layer of moss in the planting medium is dry.

At the Orchid Gallery, there were so many amazing orchids that I *couldn't* pick just one. So my mom let me choose two.

YOU CAN CHOOSE ONE!

PICK ME!

PICK ME!

PICK ME!

- USE A MISTER. On non-watering days, I use a mister to spray the air around my orchids.

- FEED YOUR ORCHID WEEKLY but with an orchid fertilizer that's diluted according to the package directions.

## PROTECT ORCHIDS BY PROTECTING RAIN FORESTS

There are more than 25,000 species of orchids in the world, which is more than mammals and birds combined! Sadly, though, many of them are ENDANGERED.

Most orchids you see in stores are not endangered or taken from the wild. However, threats to wild orchids include HABITAT LOSS, climate change, and poaching, which is illegally taking orchids from nature. Many wild orchids live in RAIN FORESTS.

You can help protect wild orchids by asking your parents to choose rain forest–safe products.

# BE A PLANT SITTER OR PLANT LENDER

Jeff Baldwin, owner of the Orchid Gallery, doesn't just grow and sell orchids—he also tends them for other people. He cares for orchids when they're sick or their owners are out of town. He also RENTS orchids to people who want to enjoy the beauty of an orchid for just a few days or a few weeks.

I decided to do the same thing! When my parents are having a special party or dinner, I offer to rent them one of my plants. I charge one ice pop per day. I could imagine doing PLANT SITTING for people, too—I could use the money to buy new plants!

**BEA'S GREEN THUMB**

PLANT SITTING AT MY HOME OR YOURS!

ORCHID RENTALS FOR YOUR SPECIAL DAY

TEXT MY MOM FOR REASONABLE RATES

MY MOM: 555-1212

# IF YOU LIKE THE MOTH ORCHID . . .

Try these other flowered beauties.

## BEGONIAS

Easy to care for, begonias come in lots of different varieties. I have two angel-wing begonias, and they like bright, filtered light.

## AFRICAN VIOLETS

These pretty little plants like similar conditions to begonias. Pinch off dead flowers to encourage the plant to grow new flowers and leaves.

SEE PAGE 62 FOR HOW TO GIVE YOUR PLANT PET A NEW HOME WHEN IT OUTGROWS ITS POT!

PART 3

# KEEPING YOUR PLANTS
## (AND LOVE OF PLANTS)
# ALIVE

Have you ever heard a grown-up say that a cat, dog, or guinea pig is a big responsibility? Well, this is true of plant pets, too—you can't just set down a plant and forget about it. Spend a little time each day with your babies, making sure they have enough light and water, turning them now and then so each side gets light, and of course admiring them.

# PLANT PET CARE AND FEEDING

LIKE ANIMAL PETS, EVERY PLANT PET IS DIFFERENT. That doesn't mean they're hard to take care of! You simply need to change your habits a little—and probably get your hands dirty.

## EVERYBODY NEEDS WATER

This is probably the trickiest part—figuring out how much or how little to water your plant pets. I recommend you do a SOIL CHECK every day, especially at first, to get a sense for when a plant pet needs water. To help you remember, you can add this task to something else you do every day, like brushing your teeth before bed: You brush, and then you check your plant soil.

How to do a soil check (for most houseplants):

1   STICK YOUR FINGER about an inch down into the soil, being careful not to disturb the plant's roots.

2   DOES THE SOIL FEEL DRY? If so and your pot feels light, add some water! If the soil feels damp, check again tomorrow or the next day. Keep in mind that some plants, like succulents, thrive in drier soil and hold a lot of water in their roots or leaves.

## TOO WET OR TOO DRY?

Just as you'd notice if your cat or dog or iguana is thirsty, you also need to notice the signs of thirst in a plant.

- DRY, DROOPING, or shriveled leaves, stems, and vines
- BROWN, CRISPY leaves
- SLOWER GROWTH than expected

Here's what's tricky: You can also *over*water a plant, causing its roots to rot. Having well-drained soil, selecting the right kind of pot (one with a hole in the bottom), and letting the soil dry a little between waterings will help roots stay healthy and strong.

Top signs of overwatered plants:

- YELLOW, DROOPY leaves (leaves can also brown)
- MUSHY, SLIMY roots
- SLOWER GROWTH than expected

If you think your plant might be overwatered, wait a little longer between waterings. It's usually better for plants to be a little dry than too wet.

## BATH TIME!

A FEW TIMES A YEAR, especially in spring, you might want to give your plants a bath. Just set them in a sink or tub with a spray faucet and give them a good drenching. This gets water to all parts of a plant's root system. It also removes dust from a plant's leaves so that the plant can use sunlight to make its own food—a process known as photosynthesis. Use a soft, damp cloth to dust your plants between baths.

Keep in mind that plants with FUZZY leaves, like African violets and begonias, are kind of like cats: They don't usually like to get wet. We don't recommend showers for orchids either, but you can certainly dust their leaves with a damp cloth.

## ENCOURAGE TEAMWORK

Help your plants work together, like they would in nature! If a plant needs FILTERED light, put it in the shade of a taller, sun-seeking plant.

It also helps to group your thirstiest plants together so that they're easier to water. Try setting them on a tray that you can take to the sink or tub for an occasional soak.

AHHHHHH, A LITTLE MORE RIGHT THERE!

# MAKE YOUR OWN SUCCULENT SOIL WITH VOLCANIC POPCORN

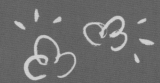

You've probably seen perlite in potting soil—those little white Styrofoam ball lookalikes are actually bits of VOLCANIC GLASS that have been "popped" (like popcorn) at a high temperature. Perlite helps plant pets by AERATING the soil, making room for strong root systems, and letting unused water drain out. Because perlite is a non-renewable resource, you might want to ask your garden shop if they have PBH rice hulls instead, which are more sustainable and do the same thing.

Potting soil includes perlite, but not necessarily enough for plants like CACTUSES and SUCCULENTS, which need really well-drained soil. Adding more perlite or rice hulls also makes it harder to overwater your plant pets because the extra water will just DRAIN away. You can make your own succulent or cactus potting soil—just be sure to do this outside to avoid a mess!

## YOU'LL NEED

* A bag of regular potting soil
* Some sand
* Perlite (or rice hulls)
* A big bucket or bowl with a lid

**1** MEASURE three parts potting soil, two parts sand, and one part perlite into the bucket. Each "part" is an equal amount—so if you use three scoops of potting soil, use two scoops of sand and one scoop of perlite.

**2** Use your hands to MIX the ingredients evenly together. Now the succulent soil is ready to use!

**3** Extra soil can be STORED, covered, in a cool place.

THREE PARTS POTTING SOIL

TWO PARTS SAND

ONE PART PERLITE

# WHEN PLANT PETS GET HUNGRY

YOUR PLANT PETS NEED TO EAT—
just not as often as furry, feathered, or
scaly pets. Their food is fertilizer. This
is usually a mix of nitrogen (for leaf
growth), phosphorus (for root growth),
and potassium (for blooms).

You can buy liquid or dry fertilizer at
garden shops. Look for plant food that
matches the type of plant you have, and
ask someone if you aren't sure. If you have
a variety of plants (some succulents and
some orchids, for example), you may need
to get a couple different kinds of fertilizer,
but each container will last a long time.

Houseplant fertilizer usually needs to be
diluted, so be sure to follow the package
directions and prepare to do some
fractions! For example, if your fertilizer
recommends using ¼ teaspoon for every
1 gallon of water, but you have a half-gallon
watering can, you'll need only ⅛ teaspoon
per watering can. During the GROWING
SEASON (spring and summer), most
houseplants should be fertilized every two
to three weeks.

## RIP TRAPPY #1

ONE SUMMER I noticed that my Venus
flytrap wasn't doing so well indoors,
where the room was air-conditioned
and low on flies. So I moved her, with
her water tray, outside to the deck into
the humid air.

Unfortunately, our neighbor's dog
thought Trappy's water was delicious
and lapped it up. He also knocked her
over into the bushes, and she fell out of
her pot. I put her back in her pot, but
she didn't recover.

Even with careful watering, feeding,
and a prime window spot, PLANT PETS
CAN DIE. It happens to everyone. Just
learn from your mistakes and try again.
Trappy 2.0 is safe from dogs and doing
great (so far).

# WHEN YOUR BABY GROWS TOO BIG FOR ITS POT

One day you might notice a plant's roots coming out of the pot's top, sides, or drainage holes. Congratulations—your plant has outgrown its pot! Like a hermit crab, she needs a new home that fits. Here's how to safely REPOT your fast-growing green pet.

1 **CHOOSE A NEW POT** that isn't more than 2 inches taller or wider than the old one. (A too-big pot could lead to overwatering and root rot.) Fill the new pot a third of the way with new soil. Stir in a little perlite if you have some.

2 **TURN YOUR PLANT ON ITS SIDE.** Holding the plant by the base of the stem, wiggle the plant out of the too-small pot.

**3** GENTLY DISLODGE THE SOIL from the roots, untangling and loosening them a little.

**4** SET THE PLANT IN ITS NEW HOME. Add potting mix, making sure to cover the roots. Water lightly.

# HOW TO REHYDRATE SUPER-DRY SOIL

Sometimes plant soil can get so dry that it doesn't hold water at all. No matter how much water you add, the water flows right out the bottom of the pot and the soil still feels dry.

First of all, try not to get to this point! Do a SOIL CHECK often (page 58) to make sure the soil doesn't get bone-dry. But if it does, here are a few tips for getting your soil to hold water again so your plant pet can get the deep drink it needs.

- BE PATIENT. Trickle water slowly onto the surface of the soil, giving it time to absorb before adding more.

- TRY BOTTOM WATERING! Sit the pot in a shallow container of water and let the soil slowly take in water from the bottom. Check on it after an hour or two, and remove the pot from the water when the soil feels damp and heavy.

- LET NATURE DO THE WORK. If some light rain is in the forecast, leave your plant outside to soak it up.

- FOR A QUICK FIX, fill up a bucket bigger than your plant's pot. Hold the whole pot underwater. You'll see air bubbles coming out as the air in the soil is replaced by water. When the bubbling stops, take the pot out of the water.

# PLAY WITH YOUR PETS
## (AND LEARN FROM THEM, TOO)

IF YOU LOVE PLANTS (and I hope by now you do), you'll want to do things with them—play with them, take them places, use them in school projects, and of course share them. Having a playful and CURIOUS attitude toward your plants will help you learn a lot from them and have fun while doing it.

## JUST ADD TOYS

If you could look closely at some of the plants in Jeff Baldwin's Orchid Gallery greenhouses, you might see something surprising—a tiny LEGO dinosaur in a hanging moth orchid, or Spider-Man climbing through the viny roots of a huge potted philodendron.

I asked him why there were toys in his plants, and he explained that they remind him of his teenage sons, who outgrew toys and LEGOs a few years ago but still have a collection. Why not perch dolls, fairies, and action figures in and around your plants?

## TAKE YOUR PLANTS TO SCHOOL

My second-grade teacher, Ms. Griffin, had a few plants in our classroom, and she let me take care of them. I watered them, fed them, and moved them to better spots. There was a cozy floor area next to her desk by the window, and sitting there and reading made me feel HAPPY AND SAFE. I set up books and a few plants I brought from home. I called it my APARTMENT, and other kids started setting up their own "apartments" around the classroom, too.

If your teacher has plants, ask if you can help take care of them. If not, ask if you can bring in a few from home. Plants make any space feel COZIER, and they happen to go great with books.

## TEST YOUR PLANTS
### (OR, PUTTING THE STEMS IN STEM)

Lots of schools these days (including mine) have a STEM focus, which stands for Science, Technology, Engineering, and Math. Plant science fits right in with the STEM classroom, and plant EXPERIMENTS are easy, fun, and inexpensive to design. Here's one we tried in my third-grade class:

- **THE QUESTION**: What's the best light for propagating pothos?

- **THE HYPOTHESIS**: Differing light conditions will produce different amounts of root growth.

- **THE CONTROL**: We took four 8-inch cuttings from a single, healthy pothos plant. Each cutting had four leaves of about the same size.

- **THE VARIABLE**: Our class split into four groups, with each group getting a pothos cutting and a clear glass bottle. We added water, inserted the cutting, and chose different spots in the classroom—a window, a bookshelf. One group chose a shady spot outside, and another group chose a sunny spot outside. Each group changed the water once a week and sketched and measured the roots.

- **RESULTS**: Try it yourself and find out!

# DESIGN YOUR OWN EXPERIMENT

You can adapt our pothos experiment for a science fair or design your own! You'll just need a question and hypothesis, a control, and a variable that tests your hypothesis.

**GOOD PLANTS FOR EXPERIMENTS:** Any fast-growing plant, like pothos

**GOOD VARIABLES TO CHANGE:** Soil composition, light source, fertilizer, watering schedule

**FUN IDEA:** You could even test whether music helps plants grow! Try searching "relaxing songs for plants" or "plant growing music" on Spotify or YouTube—or make your own playlist.

## SHARE THE LOVE

IT WAS A CHILLY DECEMBER MORNING when Andrew Pfeifer met with me and my mom at North Carolina State University to show us the school's greenhouses. Andrew was a senior studying horticulture. He was wearing a bright, tie-dyed T-shirt and shorts. "Wow, he must really like the cold," I thought. (My mom and I were both wearing coats!) But when we stepped inside the greenhouse, I understood his outfit—walking in the warm, moist air was like taking a tropical vacation.

Andrew loves plants and sharing his knowledge. "Plant people are very happy to share," he said. "If someone shows an interest, they want to help!"

That day we saw so many plants—cactuses and succulents, birds of paradise, fruiting monsteras, even a corpse plant! Andrew told us all about them, and explained that he loves BEGONIAS best because they are colorful and fast growing. He even gave us two cuttings from an angel-wing begonia. "Half the plants I own were given to me," he told us.

The best thing about plant parenting has to be sharing—not just the plant cuttings, but also the LOVE that you have for plants.

## OTHER WAYS TO SHARE YOUR LOVE OF PLANTS

There are so many ways to share the plant love! Here are a few more ideas.

- Give a friend a BOOK about plants—like this one!

- Send a POSTCARD: Cut watercolor paper or card stock into 4- by 6-inch postcards. Draw a portrait of your favorite plant pet and send it to a friend.

- Host a PLANT SWAP with friends.

# GIVE A LEAFY GIFT

We think the best plants to give as gifts are the **EASIEST** ones to grow. You wouldn't give somebody a bonsai, or even an orchid, if you weren't sure they'd love the challenge: not fair to your friends, not fair to the plants.

I love getting cuttings of cool new plants. After Andrew gave me my first begonias, my friend Marsha gave me two **PRAYER PLANT** cuttings. She presented them in an adorable, bear-shaped honey jar, and they were already well rooted. I transferred each one to a pot and watched them lift their leaves in "prayer" every night.

## YOU'LL NEED

* Scissors
* A healthy, mature plant, such as a pothos or another choice from page 25
* A clear glass jar—look in the recycling bin or at thrift shops for cute ones
* Unchlorinated water
* Paper and ribbon or twine for a tag

**1** Using the scissors, **CLIP** a 4- to 5-inch piece of stem, cutting below a node where your plant would grow new roots.

**2** **PUT** the cutting in the jar. **ADD** the water, making sure you don't cover any leaves.

**3** **MAKE** a tag and tie it to the jar.

**TIP:** Succulents are better rooted in soil than water. See page 28 for how I gave succulent babies as a birthday favor.

HI, I'M POTHOS. PUT ME IN A SUNNY SPOT, AND WAIT TILL I GROW LONG ROOTS. THEN, PLANT ME IN POTTING MIX AND WATCH ME GROW!

# PLANT MATCHMAKER!

Matching a friend, family member, or teacher with a new plant—especially one you started from a cutting yourself—is fun and rewarding. To make the perfect match, think about the personality of the person and the plant, and also consider where the person will keep the plant.

**GRANDMA** who loves to move plants outdoors and indoors

**GRANDPA** who loves to cook spaghetti

**LITTLE SISTER** who likes to use a spray bottle

*Air plant or moss terrarium*

*Moses-in-the-cradle plant or ferns*

*Basil*

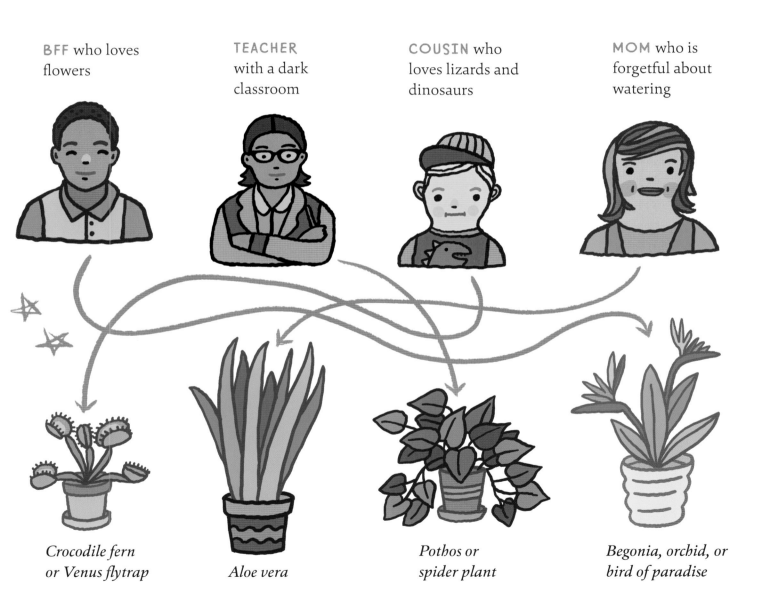

BFF who loves flowers

TEACHER with a dark classroom

COUSIN who loves lizards and dinosaurs

MOM who is forgetful about watering

*Crocodile fern or Venus flytrap*

*Aloe vera*

*Pothos or spider plant*

*Begonia, orchid, or bird of paradise*

# HOST A PLANT PET PARTY

Like clothing and book swaps, a PLANT SWAP (or plant party) is a fun, environmentally friendly way to share duplicates or plants you've propagated. A swap is also a chance to share plants that are overcrowded in their space or that you think might be great for a friend. You'll get new plants for your MENAGERIE, and you'll probably learn something new! Where can you hold your swap? A park or backyard works well.

**NAME:** MOTHER OF THOUSANDS

**RAISED BY:** BEA

**LIKES:** FILTERED TO BRIGHT, INDIRECT LIGHT. GOOD DRAINAGE. USE CACTUS OR SUCCULENT SOIL.

**DISLIKES:** TOO MUCH WATER, DIRECT SUN.

## YOU'LL NEED

* Plant-loving friends and neighbors
* A few propagated plants or plant pets you can part with (sniff, sniff!)
* Index cards and string
* Tables
* Refreshments like lemonade and cookies, music (optional but nice to have, 'cause it's a party)
* Name tags and markers

1 Making new plants will take 1 to 2 months, so PLAN this party at least that far ahead. ASK your parents to help you choose a date and INVITE some friends. The invitation should say where, when, and what to bring (healthy plants or cuttings to swap). Lots of teachers and neighbors like plants, so feel free to invite them, too.

2 GET your plants ready. Maybe your pothos needs a haircut—take some cuttings and get them sprouting on the windowsill (see page 23). Or carefully remove some juicy leaves near the bottom of a healthy succulent and set them on a tray of dry succulent soil away from sunlight.

3 Using the index cards, MAKE notecards for guests to fill out with plant-care information. Each card can be hole punched, with a string wound through the hole. Tie the cards to the cuttings, so new plant parents will know how to care for their pets.

4 SET UP a table for the plants and a table for refreshments. If your guests don't know each other, set out name tags and markers.

5 SHARE your plants and tips for taking care of them. Have fun!

# PLANT PARTY PLAYLIST

Here are some good plant songs.
Can you think of more?

* "I HEARD IT THROUGH THE GRAPEVINE" sung by Marvin Gaye

* "HERE COMES THE SUN" by the Beatles

* "GET A LITTLE DIRT ON YOUR HANDS" by the Delltones

* "EVERYBODY LOVES THE SUNSHINE" by Roy Ayers

* "DATE WITH THE RAIN" by Eddie Kendricks

* "YOU ARE THE SUNSHINE OF MY LIFE" by Stevie Wonder

* "HAVE YOU EVER SEEN THE RAIN?" by Creedence Clearwater Revival

* "WELCOME TO THE JUNGLE" by Guns N' Roses

* "SUN IS SHINING" by Bob Marley

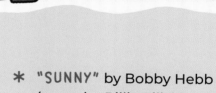

* "SUNNY" by Bobby Hebb (cover by Billie Eilish)

* "IVY" by Taylor Swift

* "COME IN WITH THE RAIN" by Taylor Swift

* "MUSIC OF THE SUN" by Rihanna

# ACKNOWLEDGMENTS

We want to thank everyone who helped us learn about plants for this book, especially Jeff Baldwin, Anju Manandhar, Andrew Pfeifer, Cindi Baucom, Marsha Gordon, Patricia Parker, and Ben Shields. Thank you to Carey Kirk for our author photos, to Jacqueline Lay and Jessica Armstrong for the beautiful book design, and to Aaron Meshon for the wonderful illustrations. Thank you especially to Hannah Fries, our brilliant editor, and the superb Kate Johnson at Wolf Literary. Thank you to everyone at Storey Publishing for sending us cool books and helping us share this book with others, and to The Plant Connector for their plant sourcing and expertise.

Thanks to all the readers of the Frog Trouble Times, who encourage us to learn new things every day. Thank you to Bea's teachers who have let her help with plants and plant experiments, especially Ms. Griffin and Ms. Tuite.

And finally, so much love and gratitude to our best and first readers: Richard Allen, Harriet Allen, Mamie and Grampa Boggs, and Nana and Grandpa Allen.